D0536269

Creatures

GREAT AND SMALL

Writer: Michael Gabb
Designer: Tri-Art
Illustrators: Alan Baker, Oriol Bath, Chris King,
Alan Male, Patricia Mynot, Nina Roberts,
Pru Theobalds, Steve Thomas, Mike Woodhatch
Cover Illustrator: Alan Male
Series Editor: Christopher Tunney
Art Director: Keith Groom

This book is available in two editions:
Library binding by Lerner Publications Company
Soft cover by First Avenue Editions
241 First Avenue North
Minneapolis, Minnesota 55401

LIBRARY OF CONGRESS CATALOGING IN PUBLICATION DATA

Gabb, Michael H.
  Creatures great and small.

  (The Question and answer books)
  Includes index.
  SUMMARY: Discusses in question and answer format the
variety of animal life from single-celled protozoa to the largest
mammals.

  1. Zoology—Miscellanea—Juvenile literature.   [1. Zoology
2. Questions and answers] I. Baker, Alan. II. Title.

QL49.   G18   1980   591   79-64386
ISBN 0-8225-1178-9-3 (lib. bdg.)
ISBN 0-8225-9540-0 (pbk.)

This revised edition © 1980 by Lerner Publications Company.
First edition copyright © 1978 by Sackett Publicare Ltd.

All rights reserved. No part of this publication may be reproduced,
stored in a retrieval system, or transmitted in any form or by any
means, electronic, mechanical, photocopying, recording, or otherwise,
without the prior written permission of the Publisher except for the
inclusion of brief quotations in an acknowledged review.

International Standard Book Number: 0-8225-1178-9 (lib. bdg.)
International Standard Book Number 0-8225-9540-0 (pbk.)
Library of Congress Catalog Card Number: 79-64386

Manufactured in the United States of America

3   4   5   6   7   8   9   10   98   97   96   95   94   93   92   91   90   89   88

The Question and Answer Books

Creatures

GREAT AND SMALL

 Lerner Publications Company ▪ Minneapolis

What are the simplest animals?

THE SIMPLEST ANIMALS There are well over a million different kinds of animals. They vary greatly in almost every way—in shape, in color, in habits, and in intelligence. Some are timid, and some are ferocious. The blue whale may be more than 100 feet (30 meters) in length. But many simple, single-celled creatures are much too small to be seen with the unaided eye.

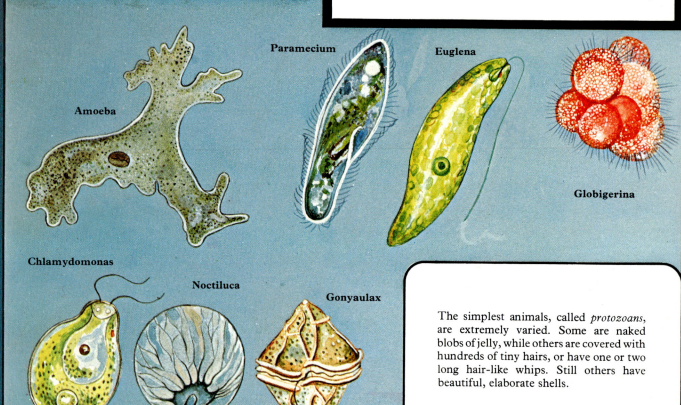

Amoeba

Paramecium

Euglena

Globigerina

Chlamydomonas

Noctiluca

Gonyaulax

The simplest animals, called *protozoans*, are extremely varied. Some are naked blobs of jelly, while others are covered with hundreds of tiny hairs, or have one or two long hair-like whips. Still others have beautiful, elaborate shells.

How do they move?

Each kind of single-celled animal moves in a distinctive way. Some animals beat their whip-like flagella. Amoeba pushes out fingers of jelly. Paramecium rows itself through the water by waving its tiny hairs called *cilia*.

Euglena moves sometimes with a squirming action.

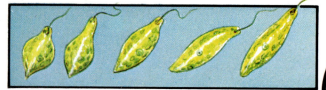

Amoeba moves by pushing out fingers of jelly, or pseudopodia.

Cilia

Paramecium with enlargement of part showing movement of cilia

Stylonichia crawling

How do they eat?

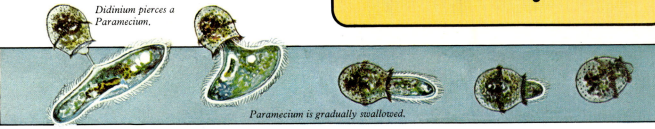
Didinium pierces a Paramecium.

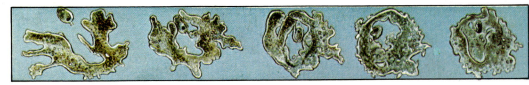
Paramecium is gradually swallowed.

Stentor

Amoeba eating another tiny protozoan

Didinium feeds by piercing and then swallowing its prey. Stentor draws tiny food particles into its gullet by beating its cilia. Amoeba flows around its food, engulfing it.

An Animal Puzzle

No one is quite sure which other animals are related to sponges. A sponge seems rather like a lot of single-celled animals joined together to form a colony. But scientists know that a sponge is really more complicated than this.

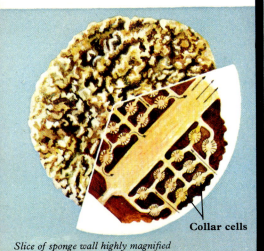
Collar cells
Slice of sponge wall highly magnified

Do they have any enemies?

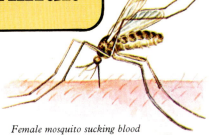
Shrimp-like creature catching protozoan

Protozoans are eaten by numerous other small animals, including other protozoans. Tiny shrimp-like animals, worms of many kinds, wheel animals, and a host of other creatures prey on them. Often, these creatures create feeding currents that sweep the protozoans into their mouths.

Are they harmful?

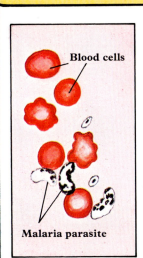
Blood cells

Malaria parasite

Female mosquito sucking blood

Many protozoans are *parasites*, living inside—or on the outside of—other animals. In humans, perhaps the best known parasite is the one that causes malaria. This parasite is carried by female mosquitoes. When a mosquito feeds, by piercing a person's skin and sucking up blood, the malaria parasite enters the bloodstream.

What are the "flower animals" like?

FLOWERS OF THE SEA Some creatures look more like flowers than like animals. They include corals, sea anemones, jellyfish, and hydras. These animals are the coelenterates—the hollow-bodied animals. Although they are simple animals, their bodies are made up of many cells arranged in two layers around a cavity in which food is digested. They live in rivers, lakes, and the sea. Sometimes, groups of them form underwater "gardens" of great beauty, hidden away where only the fishes can normally see them.

Portuguese man-of-war

There are two main forms of flower animals. One is the hollow, tube-like polyp, such as Hydra, with a ring of tentacles around its mouth. The other is the often more bell-shaped medusa of the typical jellyfish. Sometimes the same animal has both polyps and medusae—just to make matters confusing!

Jellyfish

How do they move?

Some jellyfish are able to swim freely in the sea. Others drift in the surface currents. But Hydras can move along the bottom of ponds by somersaulting. They bend over and stand on their heads. Then they bend again to return to the upright position, using their tentacles.

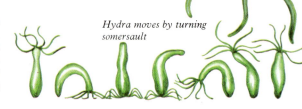
Hydra moves by turning somersault

Is coral alive?

If you watch coral carefully, hundreds of tiny hydra-like coral animals can be seen poking out from cup-shaped pits in the hard stony coral formation. Each has its tentacles out, ready to catch food.

How is a coral reef formed?

Coral is a hard "skeleton" produced by millions of tiny hydra-like animals. It is made mostly of carbonate of lime. The chalky skeletons build up year after year, forming reefs. There are three kinds of coral reefs.

Fringing reef forming around island

Barrier reef—formed from fringing reef as land sinks

Atoll formed when land has sunk below the sea surface, leaving coral reef surrounding lagoon

How do the "flower animals" catch their food?

All flower animals have stinging cells. These are used to stun food. Sea anemones can catch quite large animals such as fish in their tentacles. Other types feed by beating cilia to create a current of water. This current sweeps tiny plant and animal food particles into their mouths.

Sea anemones closed up

Sea anemone with fish trapped in tentacles

Are there many kinds of worms?

WORMS OF ALL KINDS Worms are soft-bodied animals that move by crawling. Flat-worms, roundworms, leeches, ringed worms, tapeworms, bristle worms, hair worms—these are just some of the many creatures that are included in the various worm groups. Some live in the soil, others live in water, and some make their home on (or inside) plants or other animals. Sometimes, they cause diseases. Even human beings can be seriously affected by them.

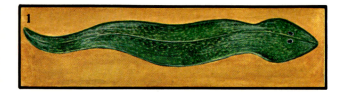

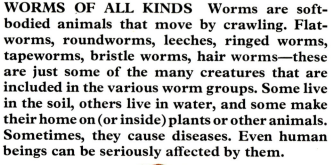

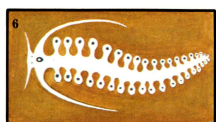

The many kinds of worms belong to several different groups of animals. They include flat-worms (1,2), tapeworm (3), earth-worm (4), the tube-building peacock worm (5), Tomopteris, a bristle worm (6), leech (7), flat worm that feeds on sea-squirts (8), bristle worm (9), and fanworms (10).

How do they move?

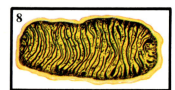

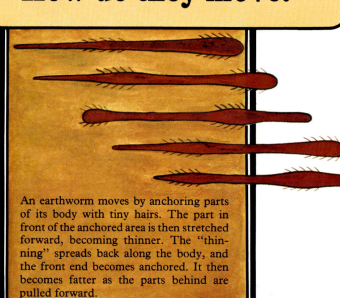

An earthworm moves by anchoring parts of its body with tiny hairs. The part in front of the anchored area is then stretched forward, becoming thinner. The "thinning" spreads back along the body, and the front end becomes anchored. It then becomes fatter as the parts behind are pulled forward.

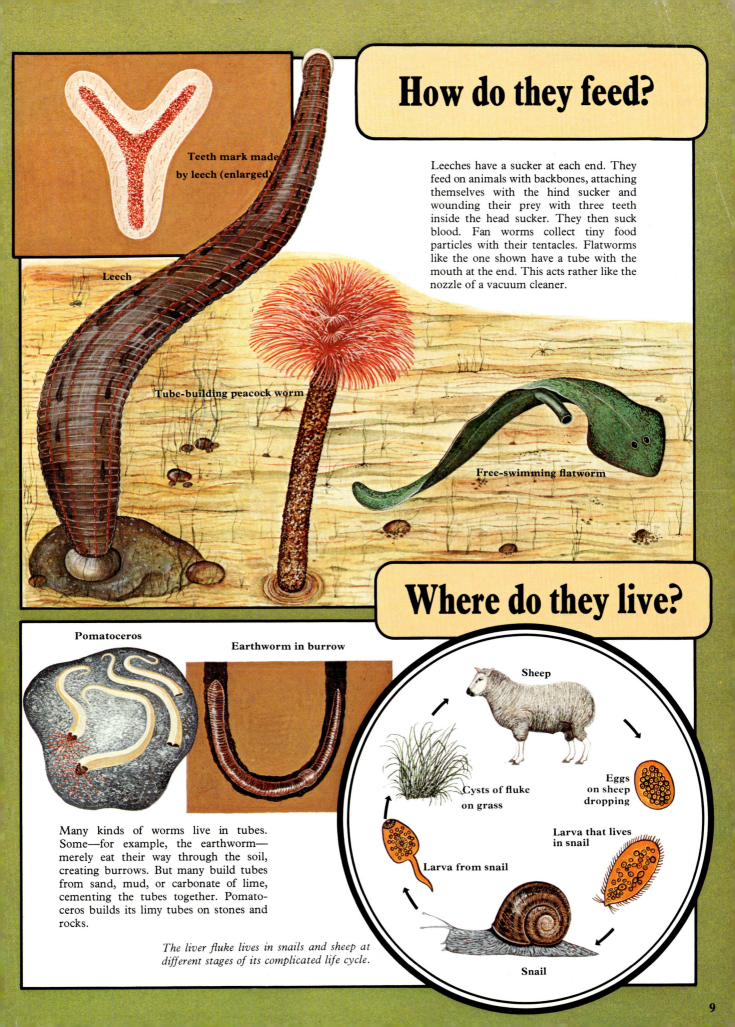

Teeth mark made by leech (enlarged)

Leech

Tube-building peacock worm

Free-swimming flatworm

How do they feed?

Leeches have a sucker at each end. They feed on animals with backbones, attaching themselves with the hind sucker and wounding their prey with three teeth inside the head sucker. They then suck blood. Fan worms collect tiny food particles with their tentacles. Flatworms like the one shown have a tube with the mouth at the end. This acts rather like the nozzle of a vacuum cleaner.

Where do they live?

Pomatoceros

Earthworm in burrow

Many kinds of worms live in tubes. Some—for example, the earthworm—merely eat their way through the soil, creating burrows. But many build tubes from sand, mud, or carbonate of lime, cementing the tubes together. Pomatoceros builds its limy tubes on stones and rocks.

The liver fluke lives in snails and sheep at different stages of its complicated life cycle.

Sheep

Cysts of fluke on grass

Eggs on sheep dropping

Larva from snail

Larva that lives in snail

Snail

Where do molluscs live?

Molluscs can be found almost anywhere—on land, in ponds and streams, and in the sea. They may burrow in sand, mud, wood or rock. Each type of mollusc has its own pattern of life. It is adapted for living in its particular surroundings.

LIFE IN A SHELL Anyone who has ever walked along a beach has picked up and admired shells of many different colors and of various shapes—some single, some double, some flat, and some spiral. The animals that live in (or once lived in) these shells are called molluscs. Their name comes from a Latin word meaning "soft-bodied." Not all molluscs have a shell, but each of them has a soft body and a muscular foot. They include snails, slugs, octopuses, and squids.

Limpet

Periwinkles

Slipper limpet shell

Whelk shell

Clam

Razor shell

Clam

Mussel

Slipper limpet shell

Whelk shell

Chiton

Wedge shell

Cockle

Mussel with two muscles

Scallop has one powerful muscle

How do they move?

Some molluscs, including oysters, move only when young. As adults, they remain on the pond or sea bottom. Clams move by using their muscular foot, and some burrow with it. Scallops have a unique way of swimming, opening and closing their shell with a strong muscle.

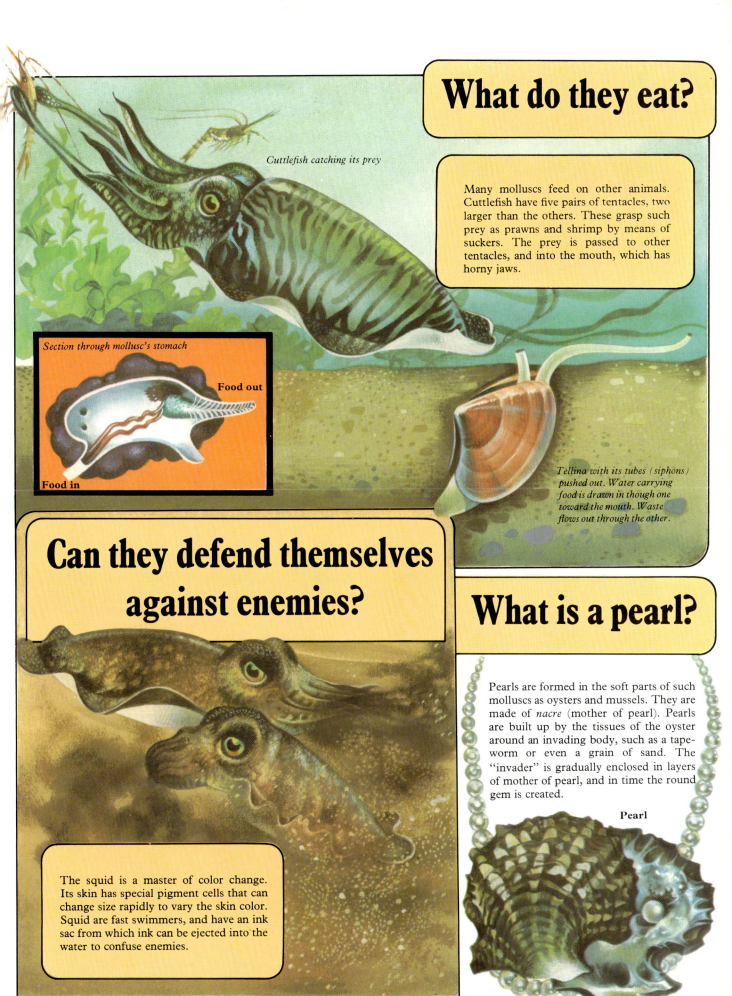

What do they eat?

Cuttlefish catching its prey

Many molluscs feed on other animals. Cuttlefish have five pairs of tentacles, two larger than the others. These grasp such prey as prawns and shrimp by means of suckers. The prey is passed to other tentacles, and into the mouth, which has horny jaws.

Section through mollusc's stomach

Food out

Food in

Tellina with its tubes (siphons) pushed out. Water carrying food is drawn in though one toward the mouth. Waste flows out through the other.

Can they defend themselves against enemies?

What is a pearl?

Pearls are formed in the soft parts of such molluscs as oysters and mussels. They are made of *nacre* (mother of pearl). Pearls are built up by the tissues of the oyster around an invading body, such as a tapeworm or even a grain of sand. The "invader" is gradually enclosed in layers of mother of pearl, and in time the round gem is created.

Pearl

The squid is a master of color change. Its skin has special pigment cells that can change size rapidly to vary the skin color. Squid are fast swimmers, and have an ink sac from which ink can be ejected into the water to confuse enemies.

Are all starfish "five pointed"?

THE SPINY-SKINNED ANIMALS Starfish, brittle stars, sea urchins, sand dollars, sea lilies, and sea cucumbers are quite different from any other types of animals. They have a basic five-rayed body plan. All their parts are arranged around a central point, or along a central line. The outer layer of the bodies of these animals contains chalky plates and spines, and, as a result, they feel rough and spiky to the touch. All of them live in the sea, and they are found in most parts of the oceans.

Starfish

Although all starfish have a basic five-rayed body plan, not all of them take the characteristic "five-pointed" form of the common starfish (above).

Serpent star

Feather star

Sea cucumber

Can they re-grow arms that break off?

Starfish can re-grow all their arms if they break off. Because the mouth and digestive organs are in the central disk, a starfish without arms can still feed. New arms will grow eventually from the disk.

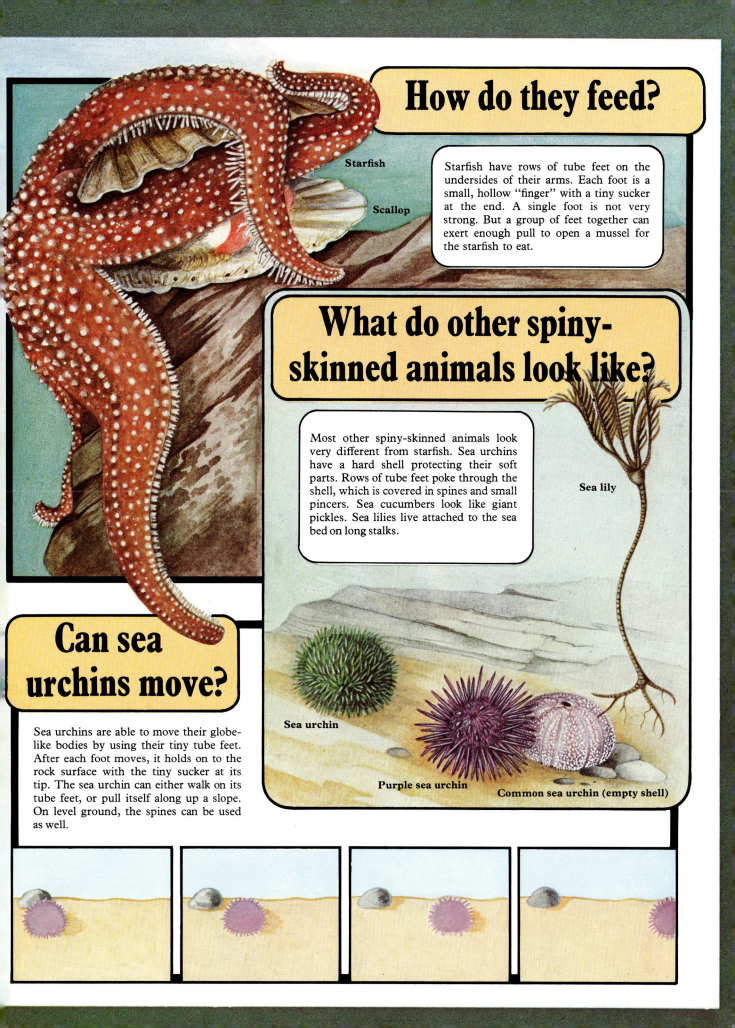

How do they feed?

Starfish

Scallop

Starfish have rows of tube feet on the undersides of their arms. Each foot is a small, hollow "finger" with a tiny sucker at the end. A single foot is not very strong. But a group of feet together can exert enough pull to open a mussel for the starfish to eat.

What do other spiny-skinned animals look like?

Most other spiny-skinned animals look very different from starfish. Sea urchins have a hard shell protecting their soft parts. Rows of tube feet poke through the shell, which is covered in spines and small pincers. Sea cucumbers look like giant pickles. Sea lilies live attached to the sea bed on long stalks.

Sea lily

Sea urchin

Purple sea urchin

Common sea urchin (empty shell)

Can sea urchins move?

Sea urchins are able to move their globe-like bodies by using their tiny tube feet. After each foot moves, it holds on to the rock surface with the tiny sucker at its tip. The sea urchin can either walk on its tube feet, or pull itself along up a slope. On level ground, the spines can be used as well.

How does a crab differ from a lobster?

KNIGHTS IN ARMOR Thousands of different species of animals with flexible, jointed shells or crusts live on land or in the sea. They are known as crustacea. Probably, the best-known members of the crustacea are crabs, crayfish, shrimps, and prawns, but most crustaceans are much smaller than these animals. One numerous sea-living group are the oar-footed animals called copepods.

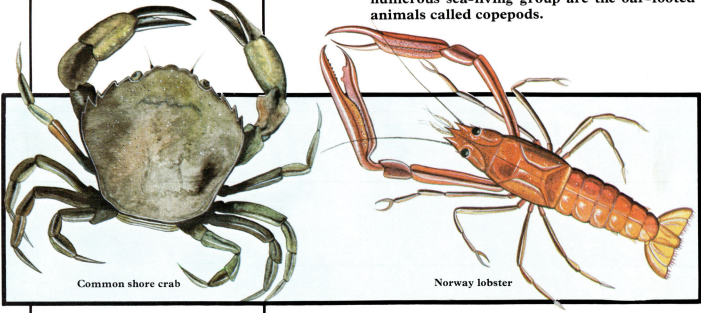

Common shore crab

Norway lobster

Crabs and lobsters are closely related animals. They have ten legs, arranged in five pairs on the underside of the chest region. But there are differences, as the pictures show. Crabs are flattened, and have tail segments that fold underneath their bodies. Lobsters have a tail fan. The larvae differ too.

How do crustaceans feed?

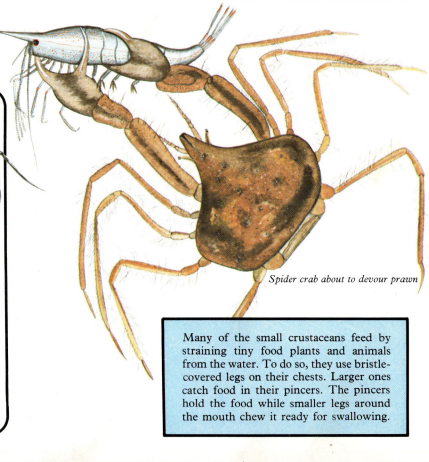

Spider crab about to devour prawn

Do any of them live on land?

Woodlice are the only crustaceans fully adapted for life on land—though some crabs, shore slaters, and others spend a lot of time out of water. Also called *pill bugs* and *sow bugs*, woodlice have to live in damp surroundings.

Many of the small crustaceans feed by straining tiny food plants and animals from the water. To do so, they use bristle-covered legs on their chests. Larger ones catch food in their pincers. The pincers hold the food while smaller legs around the mouth chew it ready for swallowing.

Planktonic larvae

Diatom

What are the smallest?

The smallest crustaceans are members of the plankton, the tiny floating and drifting animals and plants of the surface waters of rivers, lakes, and the sea. The most numerous are probably the oar-footed creatures called *copepods*, which are the main food of such fish as herring. Copepod young are also members of the plankton.

Tomopteris worm

Calanus

Scenedesmus

The Hermit Crab

Ceratium

Sea bass egg

Hermit crabs have become so well suited for life as "hermits" occupying empty whelk shells that they are liable to injury when outside their protective homes. They have to change homes when they outgrow their existing shells, and their soft bodies are then easily attacked by enemies.

Is a spider an insect?

THE WORLD OF INSECTS

Insects resemble the crustacea in having a hard, protective outer shell that is jointed like a suit of armor. They are distinctive in having a body that is divided into three parts—head, thorax, and abdomen. They have a system of breathing tubes. All adult insects have six legs. Most of them have wings attached to the thorax, and these are often brightly colored. Insects are by far the largest group of animals. They live on land and in fresh water.

If you look carefully at a spider, you will see that it has eight legs and only two main parts to its body. An insect has six legs and a three-part body. The hind part of a spider's body is not made up of sections as an insect's is. And a spider's eyes are always single units, not several.

Spider

Fly

What is a caterpillar?

A caterpillar hatches from an egg. It feeds and grows much larger, shedding its skin several times, and then changes into a *chrysalis* or *pupa*. Often, it will spend winter in this form before emerging as a butterfly. Many other insects have similar life histories. *Right*, the changes in a cabbage white butterfly's life cycle, from the time the female adult butterfly lays her eggs on a cabbage leaf until a new adult emerges.

Eggs

Caterpillar

Chrysalis

Butterfly (emerging)

Butterfly feeding from flower

Dragonfly catching its prey on the wing

How do insects feed?

Greenfly

Mosquito

Insects feed on plants and animals, and many are pests. Their mouthparts vary according to the way they feed. Mosquitoes have piercing and sucking mouths. Butterflies and moths have long tubes for sucking nectar from flowers. And dragonflies have powerful biting mouthparts, as do many ants and wasps.

Do they live in groups?

Insects that live in groups or colonies are called *social insects.* Examples are bees, wasps, ants, and termites. Each group has members of various kinds. For instance, termites may be workers or soldiers. Or their function may be to breed. Among breeding termites are the king and queen, who form the colony.

Combs of the honey bee. Eggs can be seen in some of the cells.

Section through a wood ants' nest showing the different types of individual. The queen ant is the large ant near the center of the nest.

Can they talk to each other?

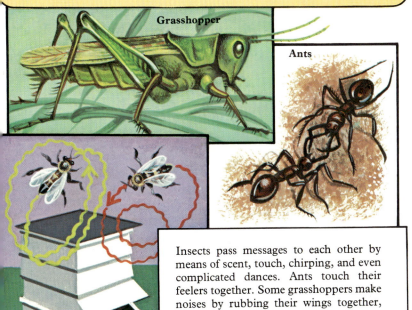

Grasshopper

Ants

Bee dances

Insects pass messages to each other by means of scent, touch, chirping, and even complicated dances. Ants touch their feelers together. Some grasshoppers make noises by rubbing their wings together, and others rub their legs on their wings. Bees perform various dances, the type of movement indicating where food is, and how plentiful the source.

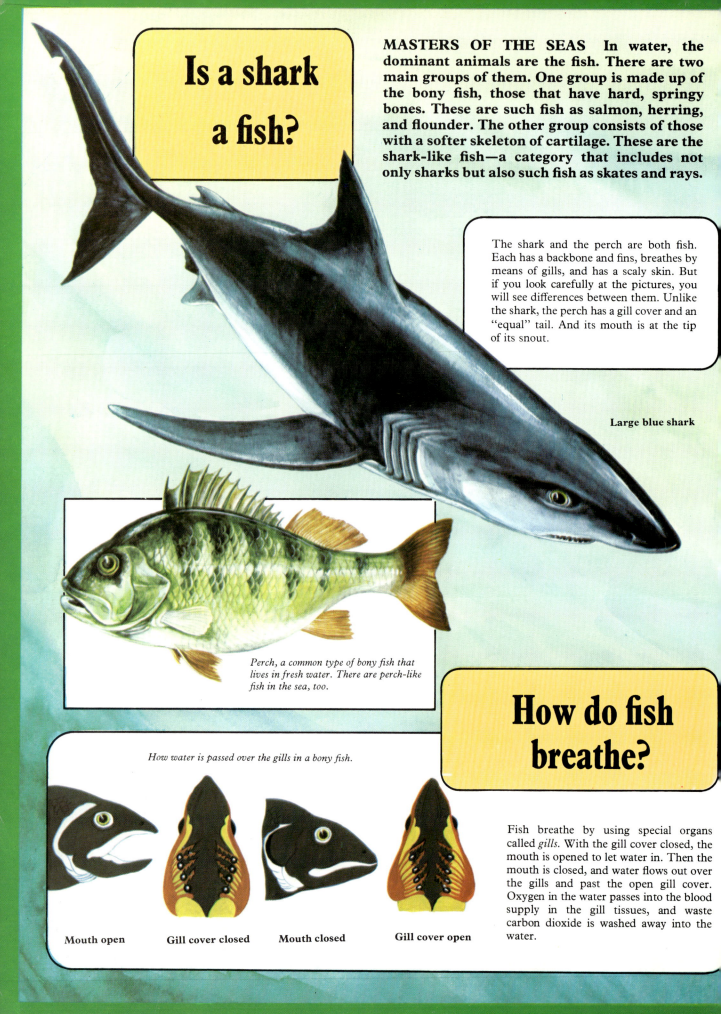

Is a shark a fish?

MASTERS OF THE SEAS In water, the dominant animals are the fish. There are two main groups of them. One group is made up of the bony fish, those that have hard, springy bones. These are such fish as salmon, herring, and flounder. The other group consists of those with a softer skeleton of cartilage. These are the shark-like fish—a category that includes not only sharks but also such fish as skates and rays.

The shark and the perch are both fish. Each has a backbone and fins, breathes by means of gills, and has a scaly skin. But if you look carefully at the pictures, you will see differences between them. Unlike the shark, the perch has a gill cover and an "equal" tail. And its mouth is at the tip of its snout.

Large blue shark

Perch, a common type of bony fish that lives in fresh water. There are perch-like fish in the sea, too.

How do fish breathe?

How water is passed over the gills in a bony fish.

Mouth open **Gill cover closed** **Mouth closed** **Gill cover open**

Fish breathe by using special organs called *gills*. With the gill cover closed, the mouth is opened to let water in. Then the mouth is closed, and water flows out over the gills and past the open gill cover. Oxygen in the water passes into the blood supply in the gill tissues, and waste carbon dioxide is washed away into the water.

Can any fish live out of water?

Several kinds of fish spend long periods on land, or can cope with dry conditions. Lungfish breathe air, and those that live in Africa and South America can survive for long periods when the rivers dry up. The climbing perch of India lives mostly on land. Mudskippers are even able to walk, using their fins as legs.

Mudskippers are able to spend much of the time out of water. Some species even climb trees.

African lungfish lives through dry season by burrowing into mud of river bed and surrounding itself with mucus. It can survive until the river reappears.

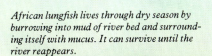

Climbing perch support themselves on land on their gill covers and fins.

How do they look after their young?

Sticklebacks with their nest

Many fish just lay their eggs and leave them to grow. Sometimes, one or both parents look after them. The stickleback builds a complicated nest, and the bitterling lays its eggs inside a swan mussel. Such lake fish as the Tilapia protect their young in their mouths when danger threatens.

Tilapia

Do they travel far?

Salmon and some trout travel long distances up rivers from the sea to breed. Eels swim thousands of miles from the rivers of Europe and the eastern USA to spawn in the Sargasso Sea, in the Caribbean.

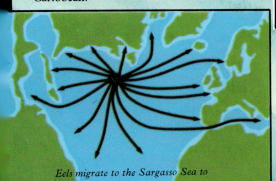

Eels migrate to the Sargasso Sea to breed.

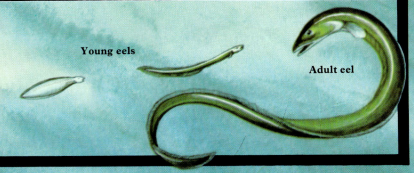

Young eels

Adult eel

Why do amphibians live on land and in water?

TWO WAYS OF LIFE The animals of one large group are amphibians—that is, they spend part of their life in water and part on land. Among the most common amphibians are frogs, toads, newts, and salamanders. Amphibians are cold-blooded animals, whose temperature varies according to their surroundings. Generally, they have a moist skin and live in damp places. They vary considerably. For example, adult frogs and toads are tailless, but newts have tails.

Most amphibians have to return to water each year to breed. Frogs and newts, for example, lay their eggs in water—either singly or in masses that form the familiar frog spawn. The young, called *tadpoles*, hatch out as fish-like creatures, and live in water. They feed on water plants, and slowly change into adults.

Adult frog

Stages in a frog's development : from egg to adult takes about 6 weeks.

Front legs appear a few weeks later

Hind legs appear at about six weeks

Rapidly growing tadpole (outside gills disappear)

Growing tadpole with feathery gills

Eggs

Young tadpole

How does a frog catch its food?

Adult frogs feed mainly on insects, but also eat worms, slugs, snails, spiders, and other small animals. A frog's tongue is attached to the floor of its mouth, and can be flicked out some distance by powerful muscles. Its tip is covered with a sticky substance.

Frogs are able to move rapidly on land and in water. The muscles of the hind legs are arranged so that the bent legs can be straightened suddenly, enabling the frog to jump or swim quickly. The short, stocky front legs act as shock absorbers in landing.

Frog jumping by extending its long hind legs. The front legs brace it on landing.

Frog swimming

Do amphibians have tails?

Crested newt

Mud salamander

Axolotl

Mud puppy

Frogs and toads, the best known amphibians, only have tails as tadpoles. But many other amphibians have tails as adults. Examples are newts, salamanders, and strange creatures with no legs called *apodans*. One giant salamander is nearly as long as an adult human being.

Midwife Toad

Male midwife toad carrying strings of eggs wrapped between its hind legs. The tadpoles develop there within the eggs for about three weeks, and the male toad then places the eggs into water where they quickly finish their development and hatch into tadpoles.

The midwife toad gets its name from the male's strange habit of carrying the eggs before these are laid in water.

How many kinds of reptiles are there?

THE REPTILES Reptiles are cold-blooded animals, but are completely equipped for life on land. They have lungs and breathe air from the atmosphere. Their skins are scaly. Most of them lay eggs similar to birds' eggs. The shells keep the eggs from drying out. Some of the commonest reptiles are lizards, snakes, crocodiles, alligators, and tortoises. In the past, in the age of the great reptiles called dinosaurs, they were the dominant animals on Earth.

Only four main groups of reptiles survive from the days, millions of years ago, when the great reptiles called dinosaurs ruled the world. These are the snakes and lizards, the crocodiles, the tortoises and turtles, and the New Zealand tuatara, which forms a group on its own. Snakes and lizards are the most numerous.

Where do they live?

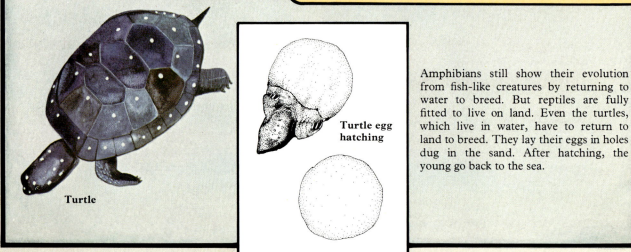

Turtle

Turtle egg hatching

Amphibians still show their evolution from fish-like creatures by returning to water to breed. But reptiles are fully fitted to live on land. Even the turtles, which live in water, have to return to land to breed. They lay their eggs in holes dug in the sand. After hatching, the young go back to the sea.

How does a snake eat?

Rattlesnake

Snake skull

Fang

Lower jaw

Pythons and some other snakes kill their prey by crushing. Vipers and most others kill by injecting poison. A viper's skull is so constructed that a poison fang is pushed into the prey as the jaws close. Because a snake's top and bottom jaws are joined only by an elastic ligament, prey larger than the snake can be swallowed.

Why does a snake flick its tongue in and out?

When a snake flicks out its tongue, it is not threatening a victim, but merely sampling the air around it. Tiny fragments of chemicals in the air stick to the tongue, and are tested by a special organ in the roof of the snake's mouth.

Can lizards really change their color?

Chameleon

Lizards have striking color patterns, and many kinds are able to change color. Chameleons have earned a reputation as masters of disguise as they stalk their prey.

Why do birds have feathers?

RULERS OF THE AIR Birds are probably the commonest, the best loved, and—often—the most beautiful of wild animals. Like reptiles, they have scales, but only on their legs. They also resemble reptiles in laying eggs that have shells. But they are unique in having feathers. Their feathered wings give them a freedom of movement that few other creatures in the animal kingdom can match.

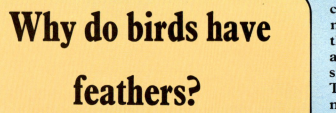

Swallow

Young pheasant

Peacock

Tufted duck

Vane

Quill feather

Shaft

Enlargement of part of quill feather

Down feather (such feathers help to keep young birds warm)

The feathers of birds serve a variety of purposes. They provide a warm, protective covering, helping to keep the bird warm. They also play an important part in flying. Their color helps both to conceal the bird from its enemies and to attract a mate at breeding times.

How does a bird fly?

Albatross

Flamingo

Birds fly by flapping their wings, and by gliding and soaring on air currents. To fly, a bird must have a large surface area compared to its volume. This is why most birds have small bodies. But the wings are comparatively large, and provide the large surface area necessary. In flapping flight, the wings are moved, not straight up and down, but downwards and forwards and then backwards and upwards. This creates a flow of air over the top surface of the wings that lifts the bird upwards and propels it forward. Soaring birds, such as buzzards, have broad wings, and use rising warm air currents. Gliding birds, such as seagulls, use the fast-flowing air currents near cliffs and at the water surface.

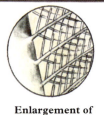

Flow of air over wing shape. Tilting the wing (right) drags the wing down. The air flow over the upper surface (left) lifts the wing upwards.

Pigeon

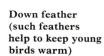

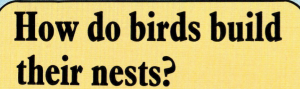

Adélie penguin has a simple nest of stones.

Australian brush turkey (below) hatches eggs, using the heat produced in a mound of rotting leaves and other vegetation.

Green woodpecker (above) drills a hole in a tree trunk.

Some birds, including the Emperor penguin, do not build nests at all. Adélie penguins have bare stone nests. But many birds construct complicated "nurseries" for their young. Mud, moss, lichens, twigs, straw, hair, and feathers may all be used as building materials.

Some perching birds line their nests with all sorts of materials, such as grass, feathers, and moss.

Are there many fierce birds?

Eagle

Owl

Secretary bird

Birds of prey have hooked beaks and sharp, curved claws for catching and holding their prey while feeding. Some, such as vultures, feed mostly on dead animals, tearing the flesh off with their beaks.

Why do some birds migrate?

Many birds migrate over long distances. They take advantage of the better weather conditions and more plentiful supply of food available for breeding in northerly areas during the summer months.

What are the main kinds of mammals?

THE MAMMALS The most advanced of all animals are the mammals, the group of animals that includes horses, dogs, cats, rabbits, elephants, tigers, and whales. Humans, too, are mammals. All mammals feed their young on milk produced by their mammary (milk-giving) glands. Generally, young mammals develop within their mothers' bodies. But some mammals lay eggs.

Horse—a placental

Monkey

Koala—a pouched mammal

Elephant

Duck-billed platypus—lays eggs

Whale—the world's largest mammal

Bat—the only mammal that can fly

There are three main groups of mammals —those that lay eggs, such as the duck-billed platypus; those with pouches in which their young grow, such as the kangaroo; and the placental mammals, which give birth to more advanced young. Most are placentals.

How do they take care of their young?

Mammals spend a lot of time and energy looking after their young. The young are suckled on milk produced by the mother. They are often carried, groomed, and protected by the adults. This is particularly true of animals that live in herds, and of monkeys and apes, which form strong family groups.

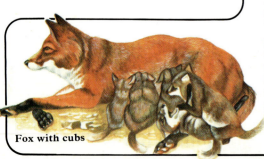

Fox with cubs

Rhinoceros

What kind of homes do they live in?

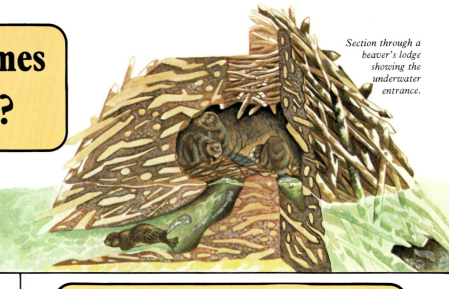

Many mammals construct nests. Rabbits, badgers, and many rodents burrow underground. Perhaps the master builders are beavers. They are able to fell trees by gnawing, and use them to dam streams and rivers, creating lakes in which to build their lodges.

European badgers have a large den underground called a "set." The nesting chamber is lined with moss and dried grass.

What do they eat?

Some mammals eat plants, others are meat eaters, or scavengers that eat almost anything. Cats and dogs have sharp teeth for piercing and tearing through flesh. Plant eaters have flat teeth for grinding. Rodents have chisel-like front teeth for gnawing.

Why do many of them live in herds?

On the great plains of Africa, vast herds of grazing animals can still be seen. They include zebra, wildebeest, and many kinds of antelopes and gazelles. By living together in large herds, these animals gain protection from their enemies, the big cats—lions, leopards, and cheetahs.

How many kinds of animals are there?

ANIMAL FACTS The variety of animals is almost endless. No human being has seen—or ever could see—all the different types of animals that exist. The insects alone consist of some 800,000 different kinds. And the individual members of each kind vary greatly among themselves. Some animals can move at amazing speed. Others seem reluctant to move at all unless they have to.

Insects	800,000
Fish	30,000
Birds	9,000
Reptiles	6,000
Mammals	4,000

There are well over a million different kinds or species of animals, and many more species are discovered each year as the wildest parts of the world are explored. Insects are by far the most common. Of the animals with backbones, fish are most numerous.

What is the biggest animal?

The largest animal ever known to inhabit the earth is the gigantic blue whale, larger even than the biggest dinosaur. Specimens of over 100 feet (30 meters) long are known, weighing over 150 tons. The elephant is the heaviest land animal and the giraffe the tallest.

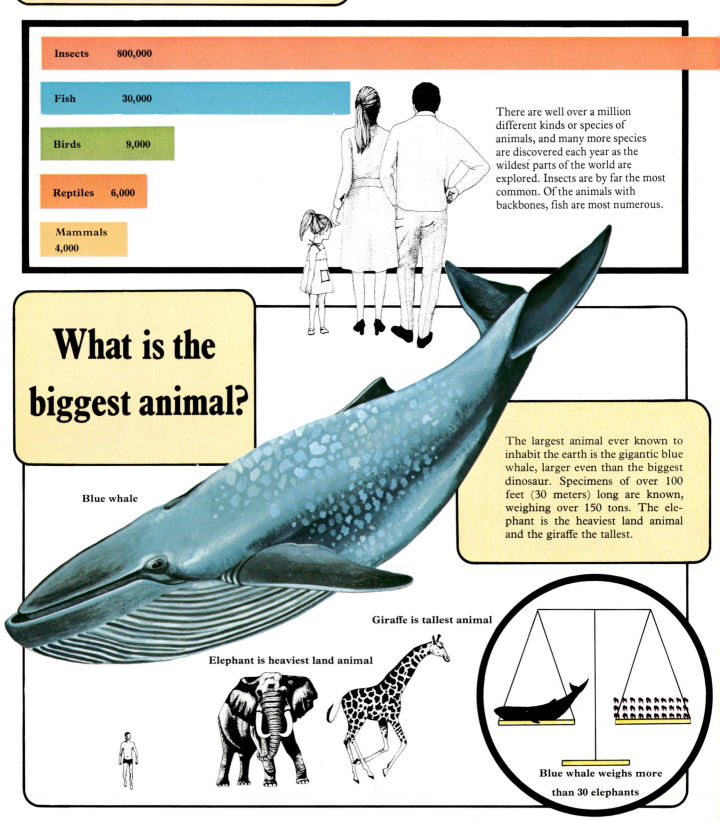

Blue whale

Giraffe is tallest animal

Elephant is heaviest land animal

Blue whale weighs more than 30 elephants

What is the fastest?

The fastest creature ever recorded is the spine-tailed swift at 106 mph (170 kph). The cheetah is the fastest land animal.

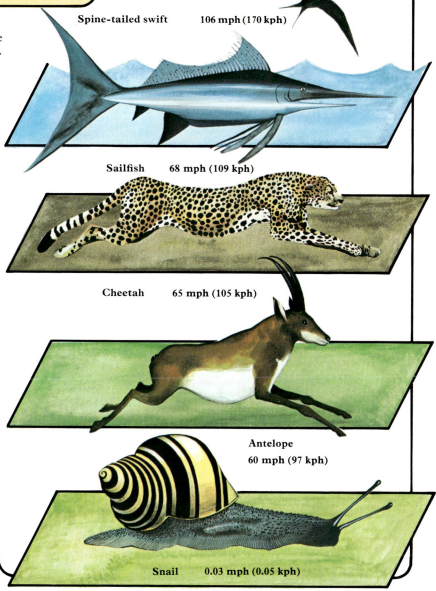

Spine-tailed swift   106 mph (170 kph)

Sailfish   68 mph (109 kph)

Cheetah   65 mph (105 kph)

Antelope   60 mph (97 kph)

Snail   0.03 mph (0.05 kph)

Which lives the longest?

Tortoise

The longest-lived animal is the tortoise — the oldest recorded age being over 152 years. Human beings have one of the longest life-spans, with 113 years being the oldest age recorded with any certainty.

Which is the greatest traveler?

Many animals migrate over long distances. Eels swim several thousand miles to breed, but birds are the champion travelers. Albatrosses wander many thousands of miles over the southern oceans, and the Arctic tern flies over 12,000 miles (19,000 km) each way from north to south and back on its annual migrations.

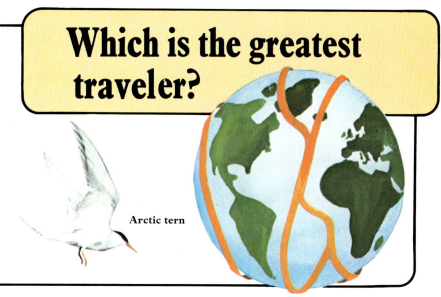

Arctic tern

Animal Defenses

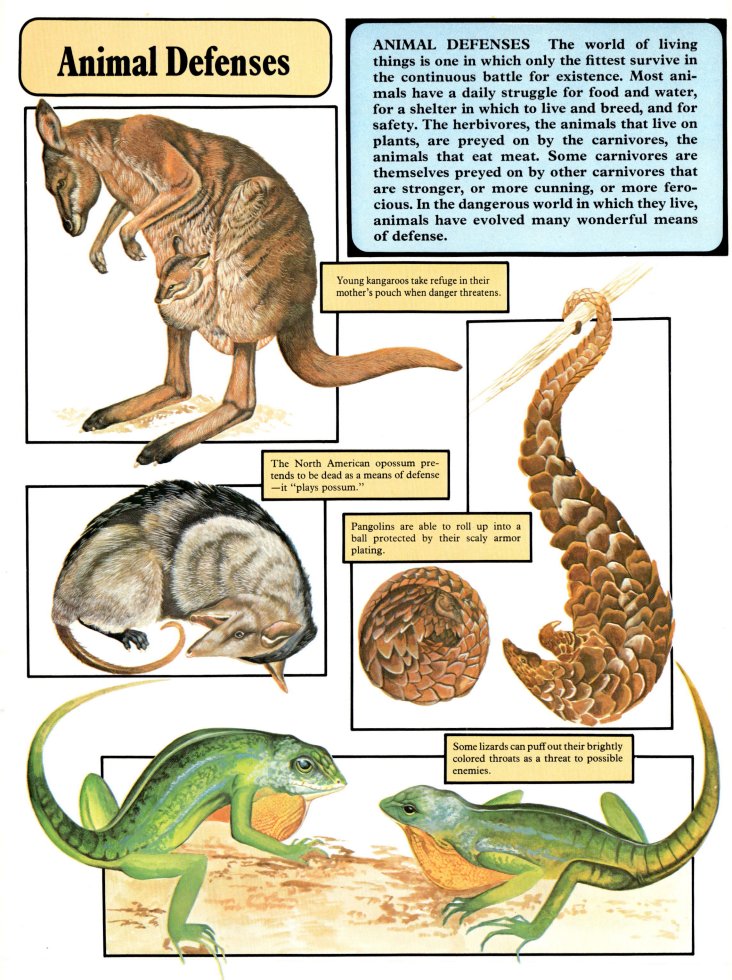

ANIMAL DEFENSES The world of living things is one in which only the fittest survive in the continuous battle for existence. Most animals have a daily struggle for food and water, for a shelter in which to live and breed, and for safety. The herbivores, the animals that live on plants, are preyed on by the carnivores, the animals that eat meat. Some carnivores are themselves preyed on by other carnivores that are stronger, or more cunning, or more ferocious. In the dangerous world in which they live, animals have evolved many wonderful means of defense.

Young kangaroos take refuge in their mother's pouch when danger threatens.

The North American opossum pretends to be dead as a means of defense —it "plays possum."

Pangolins are able to roll up into a ball protected by their scaly armor plating.

Some lizards can puff out their brightly colored throats as a threat to possible enemies.

Hedgehogs are protected by prickles. They are able to hide their soft parts when rolled into a ball.

Lizards are able to break off their tails, leaving their attacker confused while they escape.

The frilled lizard can take up a very frightening stance to try to persuade enemies not to attack.

Some moths mimic or copy other insects such as wasps and bees and so gain protection from their enemies.

A chameleon can change color to blend with its surroundings. This also helps it catch its prey.

A-Z of Animal Life

A

abdomen In mammals, the part of the body that contains the stomach, intestines, kidney, liver, and reproductive organs. In insects and other arthropods, it is the hind section of the body. *See* INSECTS; MAMMALS.

amphibians The group of backboned animals that are capable of living both in water and on land, such as frogs, toads, newts, and salamanders. They are cold-blooded. Amphibians must return to the water to breed.

antennae The feelers on the head of various arthropods. *See* ARTHROPODS.

anthropoid Like the human form.

antlers The outgrowths on the head of male deer that, unlike true horns, are grown and shed yearly.

arboreal Living in trees.

arthropods The group of animals that includes insects, spiders, scorpions, crustaceans, centipedes, and millipedes. It is the largest division of the animal kingdom, containing about 80 per cent of all animal species. The body of an arthropod is made up of a row of similar parts, called segments. It has no backbone.

B

benthos The animals and plants that live on the sea or lake floor. For example, corals and sponges.

binomial system The method of naming animals in which each type of animal is given two Latin names. The first is the generic name (genus). It always begins with a capital letter. The second is the specific name (species). For example, the domestic dog is called *Canis familiaris*; that is, the domestic dog is a species of the genus *Canis*. *See* CLASSIFICATION; GENUS; LINNAEUS, CAROLUS; SPECIES.

bivalves The molluscs whose shells have two parts, usually hinged together. The most common examples are the edible molluscs, such as clams, mussels, oysters, and scallops. *See* MOLLUSCS.

C

carnivores The group of mainly flesh-eating mammals. The word is also used to mean *any* flesh-eating animals.

carrion Dead and rotting flesh which is eaten by scavengers, such as vultures.

cell The basic structural unit from which all living things are built. A cell may be a complete living package, capable of feed-ing, growing, and often of reproducing and even moving independently. In many-celled animals, there are several different types of cell, each of which has a particular job to do—for example, blood cells, bone cells, and nerve cells.

chrysalis The resting or pupa stage of a developing butterfly or moth, which occurs between its larva or caterpillar stage and its adult form. *See* LARVA; METAMORPHOSIS; PUPA.

classification The sorting or division of the animal and plant kingdoms into groups of animals with common characteristics. These groups range from the simple major divisions to the more detailed, and are arranged in an order to form a kind of family tree, as follows: phylum, class, order, family, genus, species. *See* BINOMIAL SYSTEM; GENUS; SPECIES.

coelenterates The group of animals that have a hollow body made of two layers of cells. They are the simplest animals that have nerve cells. Hydra, sea anemones, jellyfishes, and corals are coelenterates.

cold-blooded Animals whose body temperature changes with the temperature of their surroundings are said to be *cold-blooded*. The cold-blooded animals are fishes, amphibians, reptiles, and all the invertebrates. *See* WARM-BLOODED.

crustaceans The group of arthropods that includes lobsters, crabs, shrimps, crayfish, waterfleas, barnacles, and wood-lice. The majority of the 36,000 known species live in water. Woodlice are land crustaceans. Crustaceans have two pairs of antennae and breathe, like fish, through gills. *See* ARTHROPODS.

D

Darwin, Charles Robert (1809–82) English naturalist who put forward the theory of evolution based on natural selection in his book *The Origin of the Species*. *See* EVOLUTION.

digestion The process by which the food eaten by an animal is broken down into chemicals that are easily absorbed by the animal. *See* RESPIRATION.

E

ecdysis The shedding of the hard outer casing or cuticle in young arthropods to allow for growth. A new larger cuticle forms.

ecology The study of communities of animals and plants and the ways in which they depend on one another and react to changes in their environments.

embryo An unborn animal in the process of development from the fertilized egg. It may be, for example, a chick inside its shell, or a young mammal inside its mother's womb. *See* FETUS.

evolution The process by which living things have developed from earlier simpler forms, and have become adapted to their environments. Evolution involves gradual change over very long periods of time, in some cases many millions of years. The idea was first put forward as a scientific proposition by Charles Darwin and Alfred Wallace.

F

fauna The animals of a particular region or of a certain geological period.

fertilization The joining of a male sex cell (*sperm*) to a female sex cell (*egg* or *ovum*) to produce a new individual.

fetus The embryo of a mammal in which all the main features, such as limbs, are recognizable. *See* EMBRYO.

food chain Flesh-eating animals eat other animals, which themselves feed either on other animals or on plants. But sooner or later, this process ends with plant-eating animals and plants. These food relationships in animal communities are called *food chains*.

fossil The preserved remains of an animal or plant that existed long ago. Most fossils are found in rocks, and are themselves filled with minerals which make them hard and stony. The age of a fossil is estimated from the layer of rock in which it is found. Fossils provide valuable information about early forms of life. *See* GEOLOGICAL PERIODS.

G

gasteropods The molluscs which have a flat sticky "foot" supporting the rest of the body. Gasteropods include snails, limpets, whelks, periwinkles, and slugs. Gasteropods are found on land and in water. *See* MOLLUSCS.

genus A group of closely related species of animals, all of which are given the same generic (group) name. *See* BINOMIAL SYSTEM; SPECIES.

geological periods The history of the Earth from its formation is divided into a number of periods based on the dates (in years before the present) at which major changes in the Earth's structure occurred.

H

habitat The place or environment in which an animal lives.

herbivore Any animal that feeds on plants.

heredity The way in which physical and mental characteristics are passed from parents to their offspring. *See* MENDEL, GREGOR.

hermaphrodite An animal which has both male and female reproductive organs in itself but cannot fertilize its own eggs. Earthworms are hermaphrodites.

hibernation The way some animals survive the winter conditions of extreme cold and food shortages by hiding away in specially prepared shelters. They fall into a very deep sleep, which lasts through the winter.

hybrid An animal resulting from the mating of two different species. Normally, a hybrid is unable to reproduce. A mule is the hybrid produced by the mating of a horse with a donkey.

I

imago The final or adult stage of an insect. *See* METAMORPHOSIS.

insectivores The group of small mammals that feed on insects, spiders, worms, and other small invertebrates. Moles, hedgehogs, and shrews are the main insectivores. The smallest living mammal is the Etruscan pygmy shrew, 2 to 3 inches (5 to 8 cm) long, including its tail.

insects These belong to the group of animals called *arthropods*. The body of an insect has three main parts: head, thorax, and abdomen. Most insects have three pairs of legs and one pair of antennae. Many have either one or two pairs of wings. Most insects live on land. All insects develop by the process called metamorphosis. There are over 800,000 named species of insects, which is about three-quarters of all animal species. Beetles form the largest group of insects with over 300,000 described species. *See* ARTHROPODS; METAMORPHOSIS.

instincts The forms of behavior that are born in an animal. Instinct tells an animal how to act in a particular situation without any necessity for learning what to do.

invertebrates All animals without backbones. The majority of animals are invertebrates. Examples are worms, insects, spiders, and octopuses. *See* VERTEBRATES.

L

larva The early form of an animal which has hatched from an egg and is quite unlike the adult. Certain insects, for example, lay eggs that hatch into larvae. The tadpole is the larval form of amphibians, such as the frog, toad, and newt. *See* METAMORPHOSIS; NYMPH.

Linnaeus, Carolus (1707–78) Swedish botanist who introduced the system of naming different types of plant and animal with two Latin terms, so that each can be clearly identified. *See* BINOMIAL SYSTEM; GENUS; SPECIES.

Lyell, Charles (1797–1875) Scottish geologist who first explained, in his book *Principles of Geology*, that rocks are arranged in layers (*strata*), and that the bottom layers are the oldest. *See* GEOLOGICAL PERIODS.

M

mammals The group of backboned animals whose young suckle on milk produced by their mothers. In most types of mammal, the young are born alive from inside the mother. But the most primitive mammals, duck-billed platypus and spiny anteater, lay shelled eggs. Mammals are warm-blooded and most species have a covering of hair. Most mammals live on the land, but some, such as whales and seals, live in the sea. Bats are the only mammals that can fly. The largest of all animals is the blue whale, over 100 feet (30 meters) in length and weighing over 100 tons. *See* INSECTIVORES; PRIMATES; UNGULATES.

marsupials The group of mammals whose females have pouches on their abdomens. They include the kangaroo, wallaby, wombat, and koala. A marsupial is born at an early stage in its development, and crawls unaided into its mother's pouch. There, it completes its development, attached to a nipple through which it gets milk.

Mendel, Gregor Johann (1822–84) Austrian monk and scientist who showed, mainly through his experiments on garden peas, how characteristics are passed from one generation to another.

metamorphosis The series of changes by which a larval form of an animal becomes an adult. Insects and amphibians undergo metamorphosis—for example, the change from caterpillar to butterfly or moth, and the change from tadpole to frog. *See* CHRYSALIS; IMAGO; LARVA; NYMPH; PUPA.

migration The regular and instinctive movement of animals from one place to another. Usually, the animals are moving between their summer and winter homes, or to and from their breeding grounds. Examples are swallows moving north in summer, and fishes swimming to spawning grounds.

mimicry The likeness of one species of animal to another species, or to some other object, so that protection or some other benefit is gained. The mimics may copy shape, color, or distinctive markings of the model (the original animal or object). The likeness is improved over many generations by natural selection. For example, a drone fly, which is harmless, mimics a bee to get protection. *See* WARNING COLORATION.

molluscs The group of animals that have a soft body without segments. They also have no backbone. The body is surrounded with a fold of skin, called the *mantle*. Many molluscs are protected by a shell. Molluscs include slugs and snails, clams, mussels, and oysters, squids, and octopuses. *See* BIVALVES; GASTEROPODS.

N

natural selection Darwin's theory that the animals best suited to an environment are more likely to survive and to reproduce. That is, there is "survival of the fittest." Over a long period of time, the conditions in an environment change, and the animals in that environment also change as they adapt to the new conditions. From this gradual process of change, new species of animals develop from the old. *See* DARWIN, CHARLES; EVOLUTION.

nekton Water animals that swim freely, as opposed to bottom-living benthos and floating plankton. *See* BENTHOS; PLANKTON.

nymph With certain insects, such as the dragonfly, the egg hatches out into a nymph that resembles the adult. *See* METAMORPHOSIS.

O

organ A part of an animal's body made up of various tissues that work together to do a particular job.

organism A living thing capable of growth and reproduction.

P

parasite An organism that lives on or inside another organism, which is called the *host*. The parasite takes food from the host but gives nothing in return. The host is not necessarily killed by the parasite.

placenta The specially formed organ in the womb of a mammal that enables oxygen, food, and waste products to pass between the embryo and the mother. The placenta is expelled after the birth of the baby animal.

plankton The tiny animals and plants that live and float freely near the surface of natural waters. It is the basic source of food in water life.

predator An animal that hunts, kills, and eats other animals.

primates The group of mammals that includes apes and monkeys, and also a few smaller animals, such as bushbabies, lemurs, and lorises. Humans, too, are primates. Primates' hands and feet can grasp. Many primates live in trees. Some monkeys have a gripping (prehensile) tail, which they use as a fifth limb when climbing or performing acrobatics. Anthropoid (human-like) apes, such as chimpanzees and gorillas, are different from monkeys because they have a more highly developed brain, long arms, and no tail. Gorillas are the largest living primates.

protoplasm The living material in cells. It is a complicated mixture of substances in which chemical changes are continuously taking place as a cell works. *See* CELL.

protozoans The group of organisms that are single-celled, such as amoeba. They occur in soil and water, and many species live as parasites in other animals. Some cause severe tropical diseases in humans.

pupa The resting stage through which certain insects pass while they change from larvae into adults. *See* LARVA.

R

reproduction The whole process of producing a new individual of a species. There are two types of reproduction: sexual and asexual. Sexual reproduction involves the joining of male and female sex cells. In asexual reproduction, there are no special cells; pieces of the parent break away and grow into new individuals. Some single-celled animals reproduce by simply splitting into two equal new cells. *See* FERTILIZATION; HERMAPHRODITE.

reptiles A group of backboned animals, most of which have dry scaly skins and lay shelled eggs. Snakes, lizards, crocodiles, alligators, tortoises, and turtles are reptiles. Reptiles are cold-blooded.

respiration The series of chemical processes that takes place in an animal to release energy from its food materials. Respiration involves getting oxygen from the surrounding air or water, taking the oxygen to where it is needed, and then combining it with the food materials to release energy and waste products.

ruminants Plant-eating mammals that chew the cud. That is, unchewed food is swallowed, partly digested, brought back into the mouth (regurgitated), and then thoroughly chewed before being passed back into the stomach. Ruminants include antelopes, cattle, deer, giraffes, and sheep. *See* UNGULATES.

S

skeleton The hard, supporting part found in many animals, which also gives protection and provides firm attachment for the muscles. There are two types of skeleton: exoskeleton and endoskeleton. An exoskeleton is on the outside of the body; an endoskeleton is inside. The hard casings of arthropods are exoskeletons.

species A group of animals that share a great many characteristics and can usually breed among themselves. They cannot normally breed with other species to produce fertile offspring. Species is the smallest unit of classification normally used, although it may be divided into subspecies, races, or varieties. *See* BINOMIAL SYSTEM.

sponges One of the most primitive forms of many-celled animals. Most sponges live in the sea. All sponges are attached to shells or rocks.

symbiosis A close association between two animals of different species that helps both of them. For example, the egret, which lives on or close to the rhinoceros, eats insects stirred up by the rhinoceros's hoofs. In return, when the bird is disturbed, the rhinoceros is warned of possible danger.

T

territory An area ruled by an animal or family of animals, especially for the purpose of breeding. Rival male animals stake out their territories by calling, singing, displaying bright colors, leaving a smell, or some show of strength.

thorax In mammals, the thorax is the part of the body that contains the heart and the lungs. In insects and other arthropods, the thorax is the middle part of the body, between the head and the abdomen. *See* INSECTS; MAMMALS.

U

ungulates The mammals with hoofs. They are plant-eating animals. There are three groups of ungulates: even-toed and odd-toed, and another that includes elephants. Deer, sheep, cattle, pigs, giraffes, and hippopotamuses are even-toed. Horses, tapirs, and rhinoceroses are odd-toed. Most even-toed ungulates are ruminants, and have outgrowths on their heads: antelopes and cattle, for example, have horns; deer have antlers.

V

vector An animal that carries a disease-causing organism from one animal to another. For example, the blood-sucking tsetse fly is the vector of the parasite that causes sleeping sickness.

vertebrates The group of animals with backbones. They also have an entire skeleton made of bone or cartilage. Vertebrates include amphibians, birds, fishes, mammals, and reptiles. *See* INVERTEBRATES.

W

Wallace, Alfred Russel (1823–1913) Naturalist who supported Darwin's theory of evolution. Wallace had independently offered a similar theory at about the same time. *See* DARWIN, CHARLES.

warm-blooded Animals that can keep their body temperature constant, regardless of the outside temperature, are said to be warm-blooded. Only mammals and birds are warm-blooded. *See* COLD-BLOODED.

warning coloration The distinctive colors or markings on animals that predators find unpleasant to eat. Some harmless animals gain protection by mimicking the coloration of distasteful animals. *See* MIMICRY.

Y

yolk The store of food in the eggs of most animals.

Index

Lerner Publications Company
241 First Avenue North, Minneapolis, Minnesota 55401